My First
Garden Book

My First Garden Book

WRITER
ALBIE CELFE

ILLUSTRATOR
MITZI MCCARTHY

PHOTOGRAPHERS
ALAN COPELAND AND BARRY SHAPIRO

LAWN & GARDEN

Acquisition, Development and Production Services by BMR, Corte Madera, CA

Acquisition: JACK JENNINGS, BOB DOLEZAL

Series Concept: BOB DOLEZAL

Developmental Editing: BOB DOLEZAL

Cover Design: KAREN EMERSON

Cover Art: BUNNY CARTER

Interior Art: MITZI MCCARTHY

Photographic Director: ALAN COPELAND

Copy Editing: JANET REED

Typography and Page Layout: BARBARA GELFAND

Horticulturist and Site Scout: PEGGY HENRY

Color Separations: PREPRESS ASSEMBLY INCORPORATED

Printing and Binding: PENDELL PRINTING INC.

Production Management: THOMAS E. DORSANEO, JANE RYAN

Film: FUJI VELVIA

Library of Congress Catalog-in-Publication Data
Calfe, Albie.
    My first garden book / writer, Albie Calfe; photographers, Alan Copeland and Barry Shapiro, illustrator, Mitzi McCarthy.
      p. cm.
    Includes index.
    Summary: An introduction to gardening which includes stories, games, and craft activity.
      ISBN: 1-880281-05-8
      1. Gardening—Juvenile literature. 2. Nature craft—Juvenile literature. [1. Gardening. 2. Nature craft. 3. Handcraft.] I. Copeland, Alan. II. Shapiro, Barry. III. McCarthy, Mitzi. IV. Title.
[SB457.C45 1992]
635—dc20

                                 92-26412
                                      CIP
                                      AC

92   93   94   95   10   9   8   7   6   5   4   3   2

MY FIRST GARDEN BOOK

Your First Garden Book

Here's a garden book that's just for YOU! It's all about growing things. It's got lots of fun things to do.

There are fun stories for you to sit and read, or to sit on someone's lap for them to read with you! You can even use your imagination to play all the parts in the stories. You can tell them to your friends!

There are things to do on rainy days or when it's cold outside. But the best fun starts when springtime comes and all the green things start to grow!

Your mom or dad—or another adult helper—will help you make your very own garden. You'll grow lots of fun stuff like sunflowers, popcorn, watermelons and pumpkins. There will be pretty things, too—like Strawflowers that last forever, and a pretty oriental garden for your bedroom!

You can see how to do every garden project, right there in the pictures. And all the stuff you'll need to build them in the list. Just follow the steps, and you'll be a gardener, just like your dad and mom, grandpa or grandmother!

So get started! Just read the stories and choose a fun project to do, right now!

But remember, gardens are MAGIC! So be sure to take along your imagination. 'Cause if you do, you'll meet all the characters in the stories—right there in YOUR FIRST GARDEN!

In a sunny glen lived animal friends.
 Three were bunnies with a playful trend,
one named Fluff, the others Flo and Skippy.
 And nearby lived three quiet turtles,
called by their names, Topsy, Ted and Myrtle.

Zoom! One day went Fluff , right over Ted
 and pushed him rudely out of bed.
She said, "Wake up Topsy. Go get Myrtle,
 Then we'll play, Jump the Hurdles!"

"Yes, let's go," said Skippy and Flo.
 "But turtles can't jump those hurdles, you know,"
said Ted, who yawned and rubbed his eye.
 "It would be silly for us to even try!"

"It might be fun though, to have a race,"
 Ted suggested, "Into space,
by climbing up that tall, steep hill."
 Skippy warned, "We'd be hard to chase,
but if its hills you want, we'll take First Place."

A little while later, they were ready to go.
 Flo practiced starts, but the turtles—no.
Fluff pranced on tiptoes while Skippy sprang up,
 Then the bunnies took off for the winner's cup.

Way down below, the turtles began.
 The bunnies bounced, like rabbits can.
The road climbed up, so very high,
 then all of a sudden, each bunny sighed.

Fluff said, "This isn't much fun,"
 Skippy agreed, "My feet weigh a ton."
One by one they stopped to rest.
 And all this while, it was plain to see,
The turtles raced on, quite happily.

They closed the gap while the bunnies cried.
 So stiff and sore, they tried and tried
until they gave up going higher.
 Then Flo asked, "Don't turtles EVER tire?"

Soon Topsy came to the mountain top,
 and looked down where the bunnies stopped.
"It's Bunnies nothing and Turtles WON,
 this uphill race sure was fun!"

SEED RACE TRACK

SLOWPOKE RACE

Needs: Empty, clean half-gallon waxed paper milk carton; scissors; pencils and crayons; sheet of tracing paper; paste; colored construction paper; potting soil; seed packages of lima beans, peas and pumpkins; clear plastic wrap, water.

Instructions

Which seeds will win the race to the finish line, and which will be the slowpokes?

Have your parent or adult helper cut one long side off of a milk carton with scissors. Next, carefully trace the racetrack using the pencil, and color each track a different color with the crayons. Trace each of the racing bunnies and turtles and color them, too.

Paste the racetrack to the construction paper, then paste it to the back of the milk carton so that it stands up above the carton, as shown. Fill the carton with soil and press it down firmly with your fingers, leaving the top of the soil about 1 in. below the top edge of the carton.

Next, choose the seeds for each racetrack. You can pick one bean, pea or pumpkin seed for each racer on the racetrack.

Make a hole in the soil with the pencil right in front of each racer, about 1 in. deep. Put your racing seed into the hole and fill it with soil, then press down until the soil is firm.

Next, gently sprinkle a half-cup of water onto the soil so that the seeds will swell and grow. Then loosley wrap the milk carton in plastic wrap and set your seed racetrack onto a sunny windowsill. Poke holes in the plastic.

At first your racers will seem to be napping, but in about a week they will stick their heads out of the ground. As soon as they do, take off the plastic so they can grow up the race track. The first seed to the finish line wins!

SLEEPY LITTLE DUTCH KIDS

In tiny Dutch fields
    old gardeners wield
their shovels and hoes
    and heaping barrows
beneath windmills and falling leaves.

Like little Dutch kids, named Gus and Sid,
    they plant each tulip bulb.

In rich, frosty soil,
    with digging and toil.
They'll sleep cozy 'til spring
    (and not feel a thing
of the winter's freezing cold.)

Bulbs can surprise and dazzle eyes
    with their magic tricks.

Although they seem to sleep
    dug way down deep,
they're like children in their beds.
    For in their heads,
they dream of sun and warmth.

To wake up, you know, with sprouts that grow
    and flowers of every color.

Winter's dreams will be forgotten
    in their rush of growth so sudden.
Gus's blooms turning red and bright,
    while Sid's a show-off, snowy white,
standing among their garden friends.

On every edge, by paths and hedge,
    tulips will greet the spring.

GNOME FACES

Needs: Tracing paper; pencils, crayons and color markers; scissors; tulip bulbs; tape; construction paper; glue.

Instructions

Put the tracing paper over the drawings of gnome clothes patterns. Trace them with a pencil and color them with bright crayons or markers. Glue onto construction paper. Then cut out the clothing and fold it together as shown to make a stand for your gnome's tulip-bulb head. Tape it securely. Tape scarf. Choose a tulip bulb that has a big nose to complete your gnome, and draw her eyes and mouth on with a marker. Glue it to stand on the clothes. Then glue scarf on.

WAKE-UP BULB BOUQUET

Needs: Low, flat planter dish; clean sand; tulip bulbs; plastic storage bag; water.

Instructions

Have your parent or an adult helper pick out tulip bulbs with you at your local nursery or a garden store. You'll need enough to completely fill your planter dish (about 8–12). Take them home and put them into a plastic bag, then into the vegetable keeper in your refrigerator. They should stay in the cold for about 2–3 weeks. The bulbs will think it's winter and get ready to grow.

When your bulbs have slept in the refrigerator for at least 14 days, fill your planter dish halfway full of clean sand so it is about 1 in. deep. Then take your bulbs out of the refrigerator and push them into the sand with their pointy ends up. Fit as many bulbs as you can into the dish, side by side and close together.

Add water until it begins to show on top of the sand. Put the bulbs in a warm, sunny place, in a few days, you will see a green sprout begin to grow from the top of each bulb. Revolve the planter dish a half turn every day so that the sprouts grow straight up and don't bend toward the light.

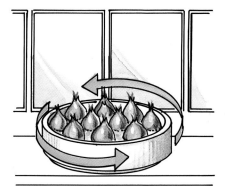

Water every 4–5 days, as needed, to keep the sand damp. In about 3–4 weeks, your bulbs will begin to bloom, making a beautiful bouquet for your house.

Idea

Plan a holiday centerpiece for your Thanksgiving or Christmas table! Put bulbs into the refrigerator by October 1 for Thanksgiving, or November 1 for Christmas.

The Princess's Slippers

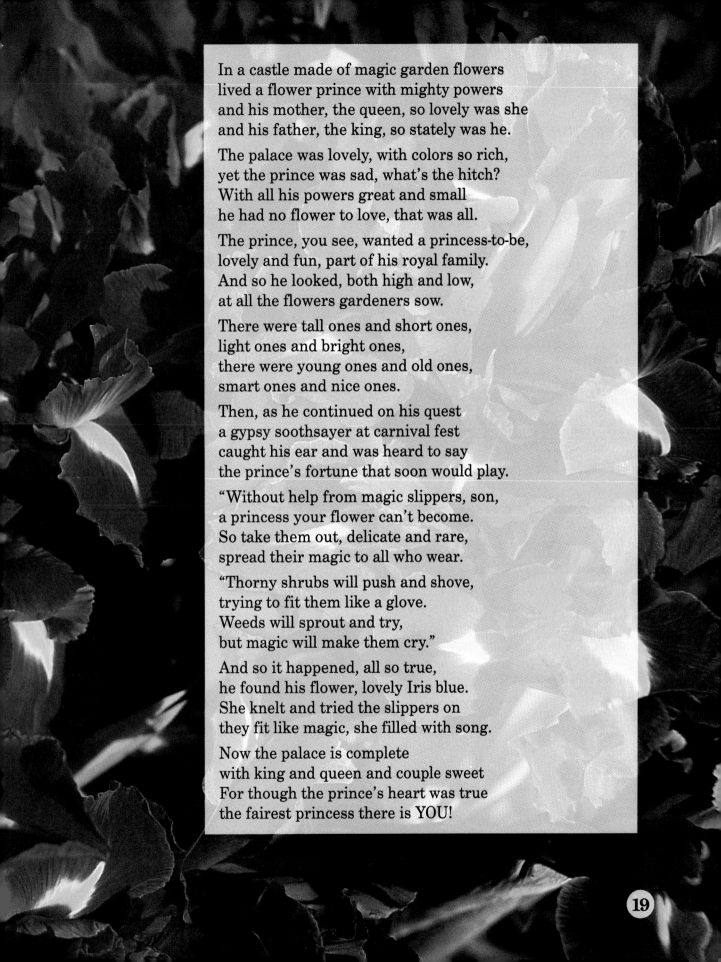

In a castle made of magic garden flowers
lived a flower prince with mighty powers
and his mother, the queen, so lovely was she
and his father, the king, so stately was he.

The palace was lovely, with colors so rich,
yet the prince was sad, what's the hitch?
With all his powers great and small
he had no flower to love, that was all.

The prince, you see, wanted a princess-to-be,
lovely and fun, part of his royal family.
And so he looked, both high and low,
at all the flowers gardeners sow.

There were tall ones and short ones,
light ones and bright ones,
there were young ones and old ones,
smart ones and nice ones.

Then, as he continued on his quest
a gypsy soothsayer at carnival fest
caught his ear and was heard to say
the prince's fortune that soon would play.

"Without help from magic slippers, son,
a princess your flower can't become.
So take them out, delicate and rare,
spread their magic to all who wear.

"Thorny shrubs will push and shove,
trying to fit them like a glove.
Weeds will sprout and try,
but magic will make them cry."

And so it happened, all so true,
he found his flower, lovely Iris blue.
She knelt and tried the slippers on
they fit like magic, she filled with song.

Now the palace is complete
with king and queen and couple sweet
For though the prince's heart was true
the fairest princess there is YOU!

FILL THE CASTLE

Needs: Tracing paper; pencils, crayons or color markers; scissors; glue .

Instructions

Put the tracing paper over the King, Queen, Prince, Princess and Gypsy. Carefully trace them with the pencil and color them with bright crayons or markers. Then cut each one out, and paste them into their place in the castle.

PLANT A FLOWER CASTLE

Needs: 3 ft. x 3 ft. flower bed; garden tools; stones or rocks; clay garden pot 10 in. in diameter; plastic straws; tracing paper; pencils, crayons or color markers; seeds: Alyssum, Pansy and Candytuft.

Instructions

With an adult helper, prepare a bed of rich garden soil (see pgs. 74–79 for help). Outline the edge of the castle flower bed with some of the stones and fill the center with 4–6 in. of soil. Firm the soil with your hands. Then make another ring of stones about 1 ft. inside the first row. Carefully pour some more rich soil in the center of the bed. Smooth it out so it is about 4–6 in. taller than the outside row, like a layer on a cake, and firm it with your hands.

Fill the clay pot with dirt and press it down. Then turn it upside-down on a corner of the center level, as the drawing shows. Remove the pot, leaving a dirt "tower" behind. Do the same for each of the other corners. Then trace the pennant designs onto your tracing paper, color them with crayons or permanent markers, and glue them to the straws to make colorful banners. Stick one pennant in each tower.

Plant the seeds as shown in the picture, with the alyssum along the lowest level, pansies on the edge of the second level and on each tower, and the candytuft in the center. Water the seeds gently, being careful not to wash away your flower castle's soil. Keep the soil damp by watering each day for the first week, and then whenever the soil dries.

In 2 months, your flower castle will be bright with your favorite flowers, with the pansies standing guard over the alyssum and candytuft.

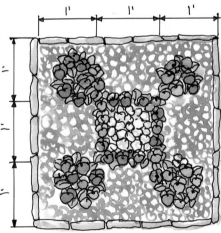

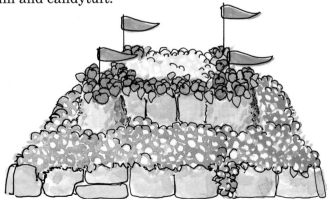

HAUNTED HOLLOW'S HEADS

Now gather round, for scary stories
    said the pumpkins in the patch.
More than shivers from frosty cold,
    these words, for you will hold.

For in the autumn, nights fill with gloom
    until we see the rising moon,
and listen in the shadows dark
    for Jack-o-lantern's voice to hark!

We don't know who carved him, oh so scary
    with pointy eyes and mouth,
candlelight pours out of every opening
    from vinetop at north to neck at south.

He tells us stories about the time
    he rode a horse so fit and fine
through the dark night to this place
    then fell down, right on his face.

Oh what stories he does tell,
    to make the little pumpkins shudder.
With ghosts and goblins they fill with fright,
    and call out for their mother!

But even though he scares us silly
    about his falling from that filly,
his stories are meant to pave the way
    for our upcoming Halloween's Eve day.

For soon, when orange from our top spreads down
    and we've grown big and round
the children will come and carve us too,
    here on the ground where we were found.

They'll hoist us high upon a sheet
    With vines that dangle like our feet
and light the candles, fat and wide,
    to make us glow deep inside.

Then we'll laugh and tell our stories
    about Jack-o-lanterns that did ride
through the haunted hollow's trails
    atop a horse, so tall and wide.

DRAW SCARY FACES

Needs: Drawing paper, pencils and color markers, masking tape, old ballpoint pen.

Instructions

Draw some 6 in. circles on the drawing paper. Then draw some scary faces that will look good on your pumpkins. Give them eyes, a funny nose and a smiling or frowning mouth. Try drawing funny eyebrows and teeth, too!

Choose your favorite drawing and take it to your pumpkin patch. Carefully tape it over a young pumpkin about the same size as your drawing.

With the old ballpoint pen, trace your scary face onto the pumpkin, pushing just hard enough to dent the pumpkin but not tear its skin. When you finish, take off the drawing and retrace any places where the face doesn't show clearly.

When your pumpkin grows up big and orange, your scary face will grow up on it, like Halloween magic!

PLANT A PUMPKIN PATCH

Needs: 10 ft. x 10 ft. garden bed, hose or watering can, pumpkin seeds.

Instructions

In early July, with an adult helper, prepare the soil in your pumpkin patch for planting (see pgs. 74–79 for help). Pumpkins need lots of room for their vines to spread out. Make 3 mounds of soil 3 ft. apart in the center of the patch, about 6 in. high and 12 in. wide. Form basins around each mound for watering.

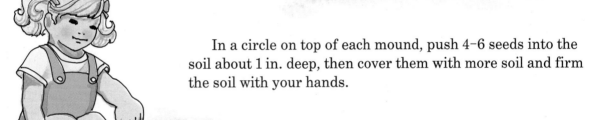

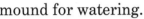

In a circle on top of each mound, push 4–6 seeds into the soil about 1 in. deep, then cover them with more soil and firm the soil with your hands.

Water the seeds gently each day until they sprout, taking care not to wash them out or uncover them. Then, water them whenever the soil dries out. The vines will soon start to spread out. Train them back into the pumpkin patch if they try to get away!

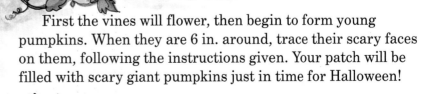

First the vines will flower, then begin to form young pumpkins. When they are 6 in. around, trace their scary faces on them, following the instructions given. Your patch will be filled with scary giant pumpkins just in time for Halloween!

From tall ships near a sunny beach
    through the jungle green was seen,
mighty pyramids of stone that towered—
    through cloudless skies, they did reach.

There once lived Aztec kings that wore
    cloaks of feathers from birds that soar
and upon the stones which they did tread
    were carved a giant sunflower head.

To the Aztec city the explorers came
    and walked its streets to meet
the king and all his court so rich,
    with parrots and monkeys tame.

There the visitors heard the story
    of when the city had reached its glory
and how the mighty sunflower king
    gave them a clock, a great, round ring.

It told the day, it told the year
    and said when summer's heat would beat.
It told when winter's rain would fall
    and when the crops would sear.

No greater wealth the city owned
    than this gift, a clock that warned
when to plant and when to reap
    when to celebrate, or to weep.

But the explorers saw no treasure
    and aboard their ships they slipped.
They had looked in vain for gold and jewels,
    but never found that pleasure.

The sunflower king, a mighty one,
    loved by his people like the sun.
His face was carved for their eyes to roam
    on his pyramid, made of stone.

SUNFLOWER FUNDIAL

Needs: Tracing paper, ballpoint pen, scissors, stiff cardboard, aluminum foil, glue, sunflower seeds.

Instructions

Carefully trace each piece of the sundial. Put a sheet of smooth aluminum foil on a soft surface, such as a magazine, then cover it with your tracing. Trace the sundial again with the ballpoint pen, pressing hard to make grooves in the aluminum foil.

Then cut out the pieces and glue them upside-down to the cardboard, folding the edges around the cardboard. Put the upright piece into the slot in the bottom piece. Decorate the outside edge with the flower petals by gluing sunflower seeds onto it.

With your adult helper, take the sundial and a wristwatch outside on a sunny day. Put the sundial on a flat surface in the sun, and move it back and forth until the shadow of the upright falls on the right hour of the day. Then glue it down, or weight it so it can't move or blow away.

As the sun moves through the sky, its shadow will tell the time on the sunflower sundial clock.

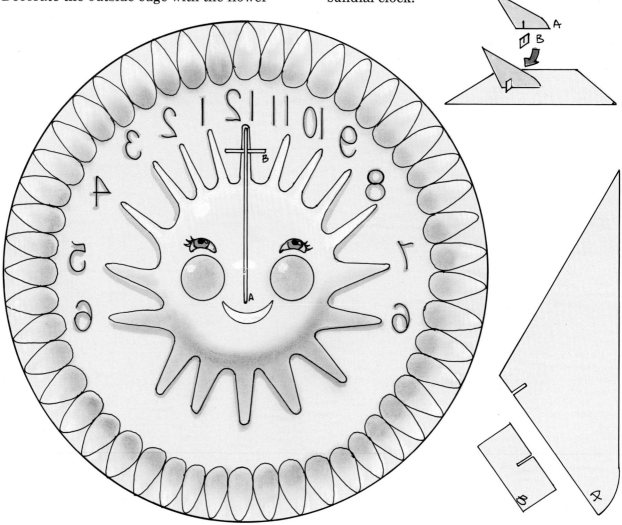

PLANTING FLOWER GIANTS

Needs: 4 ft. x 12 ft. flower bed strip, hose or watering can, sunflower seeds.

Instructions

Sunflowers grow taller than most PEOPLE—6-8 ft. tall! They need lots of space and lots of sun. Have an adult helper prepare the soil for planting (see pgs. 74-79 for help). A spot along a south-facing fence or wall is best.

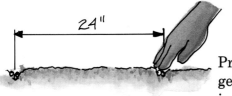

Plant 2 seeds every 2 ft., poking them about 1 in. deep. Press the soil firmly with your hands, and water the seeds gently every day until they sprout. You should see the sprouts in about a week.

About three weeks after you plant, pinch off the weakest plant in each pair, leaving just one. Be sure to water them whenever the soil dries. A big, single flower will soon form.

When the back of the flower turns completely yellow, cut the stem off about 1-2 ft. below the flower and hang it upside down to dry. It will dry out in 3-4 weeks. Pick the seeds from the dried flowerhead. Eat them raw or have your adult helper roast them for you in the oven—or share them with your wild bird friends!

BIG MUDDY AND THE RIVER RAFT

Tom fell asleep while fishing
at the river's rushing shore
and dreamt of times so long ago
while he began to snore.

He dreamt of floating downstream
on a raft made out of wood
while by his side, his best friend Tammy
caught what fish she could.

They drifted round the river's bend
and came to a secret place,
where melons ripened in the sun
and a smile grew on each face.

Tom polled their raft up to the bank
and tied up to a tree.
Tammy jumped ashore to take a look
and see what she could see.

They thumped each melon on its top
to see if it was ripe
and finally found the biggest one
green and round with stripes.

Tom reached out to cut it free
but stopped when he heard a shout!
"Stop, thief," a farmer cried at them
"That melon's mine—get out!"

They were frightened half to death,
and scared down to their knees,
until they saw the farmer's smile
"All you had to say was, 'Please?' "

"There's plenty of melons here, you see,
enough for all to share,
I've ripened them in the summer sun
to eat them's only fair!"

GROW A WATERMELON PATCH

Needs: 8 ft. x 16 ft. garden plot, shovel, hoe, rake, water hose, Watermelon seeds.

Instructions

With an adult helper, prepare the soil for planting in your watermelon patch (see pgs. 74–79 for help). Choose a site with full sun all day long. After the earth is loosened and fertilizer has been added, make two hills 6 ft. apart, each 12 in. in diameter and 6–8 in. high.

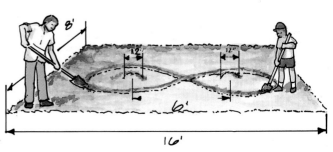

Make a "Big Muddy River" irrigation canal to go around each hill to make watering the watermelon patch easy. You can have lots of fun with this canal (see next page).

Sow 4–6 seeds around the top of each hill in a circle, poking them 1 in. deep with your finger. Then fill each hole with dirt and press the soil firm with your hands.

Water the seeds gently each day on top of the mound for the first week, until they sprout. Then begin watering them by using the water channel whenever the soil dries out or when the plants wilt in the sun.

Depending on the type of melon planted, ripe watermelons will be ready to eat in 80–120 days.

RACING RIVER RAFTS

Needs: 1/2 in. dowel cut into 6 in. pieces, popsicle sticks, waterproof glue, plastic straw, bits of colored cloth, water hose.

Instructions

Have an adult helper cut sticks from the dowel, using a saw.

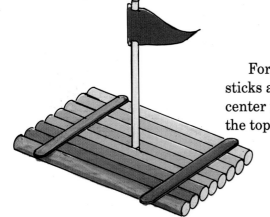

For each raft, lay 8 dowels side-by-side and glue 2 popsicle sticks as shown in the picture. Glue the plastic straw in the center for a flagpole, and cut a triangle of cloth and glue it to the top of the straw to make a flag.

After the glue dries, float the rafts in the irrigation channel of your watermelon patch. The best time to race your rafts each day is when you water your melons. Use the hose to make a current, and see which one gets to the other melon hill first!

Remember, always be careful not to wash away your melon vines at their roots or to spray the young melons with water! If you do, your melons will die or rot.

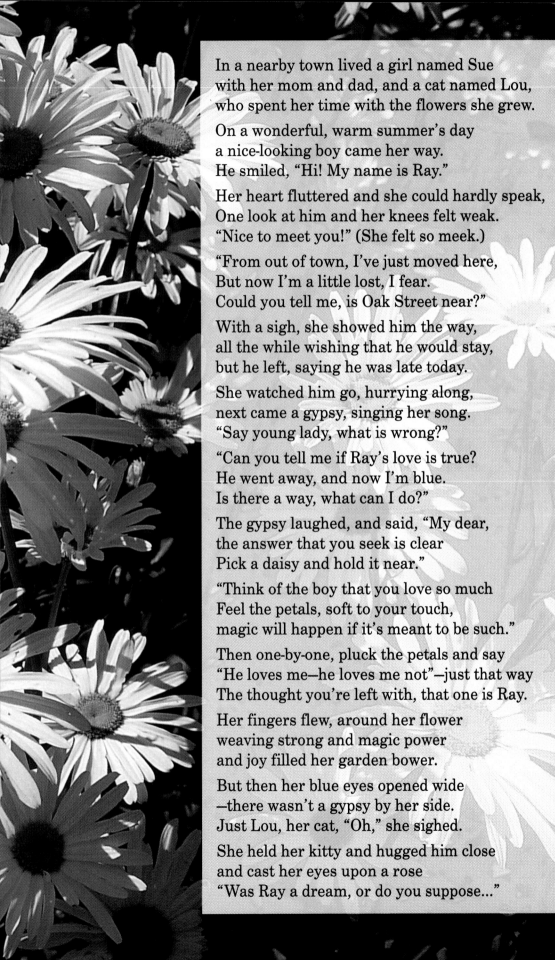

In a nearby town lived a girl named Sue
with her mom and dad, and a cat named Lou,
who spent her time with the flowers she grew.

On a wonderful, warm summer's day
a nice-looking boy came her way.
He smiled, "Hi! My name is Ray."

Her heart fluttered and she could hardly speak,
One look at him and her knees felt weak.
"Nice to meet you!" (She felt so meek.)

"From out of town, I've just moved here,
But now I'm a little lost, I fear.
Could you tell me, is Oak Street near?"

With a sigh, she showed him the way,
all the while wishing that he would stay,
but he left, saying he was late today.

She watched him go, hurrying along,
next came a gypsy, singing her song.
"Say young lady, what is wrong?"

"Can you tell me if Ray's love is true?
He went away, and now I'm blue.
Is there a way, what can I do?"

The gypsy laughed, and said, "My dear,
the answer that you seek is clear
Pick a daisy and hold it near."

"Think of the boy that you love so much
Feel the petals, soft to your touch,
magic will happen if it's meant to be such."

Then one-by-one, pluck the petals and say
"He loves me—he loves me not"—just that way
The thought you're left with, that one is Ray.

Her fingers flew, around her flower
weaving strong and magic power
and joy filled her garden bower.

But then her blue eyes opened wide
—there wasn't a gypsy by her side.
Just Lou, her cat, "Oh," she sighed.

She held her kitty and hugged him close
and cast her eyes upon a rose
"Was Ray a dream, or do you suppose..."

GYPSY DAISIES

Needs: Empty milk carton, scissors, potting soil, plastic wrap, Gloriosa Daisy seeds, water, transplant pots, 4 ft. x 6 ft. flower bed.

Instructions

Have your parent or an adult helper cut open a milk carton lengthwise along one side.

Wash it out, then fill it half full with potting soil. Sprinkle in the seeds and sift a little soil (about 1/4 in.) over the seeds. Gently sprinkle water on the seeds until the soil is moist, but not soggy.

Cover the milk carton with plastic wrap and poke a few holes in it so the seeds can breathe. Put it in a sunny window, and in 5–10 days the seeds will sprout.

When the seedlings emerge, then take the plastic off and throw it away. Continue watering the tiny plants until they are about 2–3 in. high and have at least 2 pairs of real leaves.

Transplant the seedlings into individual pots. When the weather is warm and all danger of frost has passed transplant them into a sunny garden. Each plant should be 12–18 in. away from its neighbor. Large daisies will form on 2 ft. high plants.

GYPSY JEWELS

Needs: Daisy flowers, string or sturdy thread, blunt needle.

Instructions

Make gypsy flower necklaces from your daisies by stringing them together with a needle onto the string and tying the ends of the string together. If you want to make a necklace without using string, use your thumb to split the daisy stem right below the flower, then slip another daisy stem through the hole. Pierce the second flower to make a hole for a third flower, and so on. When your necklace is long enough, join the last flower to the first one to make a continuous chain.

Use the same ideas to make lots of gypsy jewelery—headbands and bracelets.

When you have all your gypsy jewels finished, you can tell each other's fortune by picking the petals off of the daisies, just like the little girl did in the story!

37

By the elephants, big and gray
    On a happy circus day,
The lion trainer found so sad
    Two little children that had
Lost their way.

"Say!" he said. (His name was Fred.)
    "Why are you here, in my shed?

"It won't be safe, you must leave soon!
    My lions and tigers and big baboon,
My elephants and me, into the ring
    Will dance and leap, the band will sing
And play a tune."

"Oh let us see! We love the drum,"
    they begged the trainer, "Can we come?"

"Please don't make us leave! We do not know
    Where our Daddy went, and so
If you leave us all alone, we fear
    We don't know our way home from here
Where will we go?"

But just then, Daddy came in.
    He hugged them close, "Where have you been?"

The lion trainer thought and thought
    Wrinkling his brow, then smiled and brought
Big bags of popcorn, buttery white
    and found both children a seat just right
Where clowns ran by, and balls were caught

Soon the big cats, from their cage
    Came into the ring, then roared with rage.

The kids ate popcorn, nice and hot.
    The lions hopped, from ring to spot.
The elephants bowed, then raised their trunks
    The baboons danced, those silly monks!
The trainer laughed, at all he'd taught.

When the show ended, the trainer bowed
    They clapped their hands and cheered him loud.

LOST AT THE CIRCUS GAME

Needs: Sheet of paper, paper cup, bowl of popped popcorn.

Rules

Two or more can play. Have your parent or adult helper pop a bowl of popcorn. Draw a circle on a piece of paper using a paper cup as a guide. Count out five pieces of unpopped popcorn and put them into the paper cup. Pick another corn kernel for each player as as marker and put it on Start.

The first one to get to the circus in the center of the maze wins the game and gets to eat the bowl of popcorn.

Who goes first? With eyes covered, each player picks up the cup with the corn kernels and dumps it onto the paper. The one with the highest number of kernels in the circle goes first. Then the player to the right goes, and so on.

On your turn, put the five kernels into the cup and close your eyes, then dump them onto the circle. You get to move the same number of squares as the number of kernels you got into the circle. You can move in any direction, as long as you don't leave the maze. The circus wagon blocks your way.

Try to avoid the Lions and Tigers. If you land on one, you have to go back to Start and begin again. If you land on an Elephant or Baboon, you get another free turn. And, if you land on the Lion Trainer, go right to the circus!

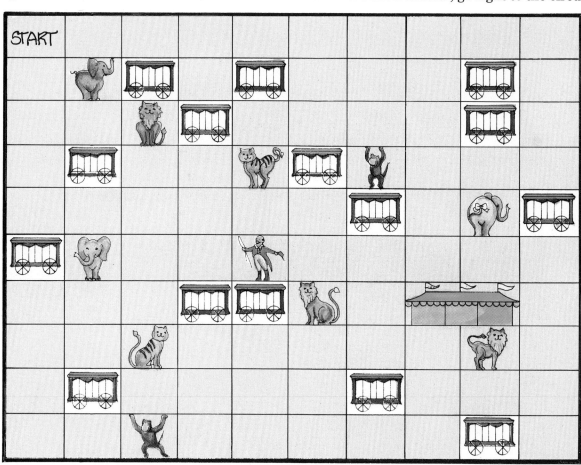

40

POPCORN GARDEN

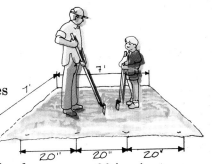

Needs: Full sun garden at least 7 ft. x 7 ft., popcorn seeds.

Instructions

Have your parent or adult helper show you how to prepare your garden soil for planting (see pgs. 74–79 for help). The best time to plant is in early June, but those in warm climates may be able to start as early as April.

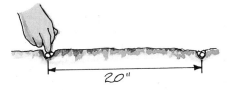

Plant 3 corn kernels, 1 in. deep, every 20 in., in 4 rows so that the plantings make a big square. Water them gently with a hose or watering can each day until the tiny popcorn plants come up through the soil. Be patient, because it will take about 2 weeks.

When the popcorn is 3 in. tall, pull out the extras so that just two stalks are in each hole.

Then watch! The corn will probably grow taller than you are! After the ears of popcorn grow on the stalks and the plants have all dried out (about 3 months from planting), you can pick off the popcorn ears.

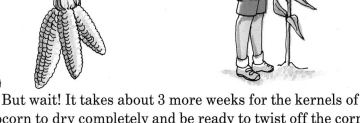

But wait! It takes about 3 more weeks for the kernels of popcorn to dry completely and be ready to twist off the corn cobs. Pull the husks backward off of the ear, and keep them in a warm, dry place.

When the kernels twist off of the cob easily, you can pop your own popcorn and eat it, just like the kids in the Lost at the Circus story!

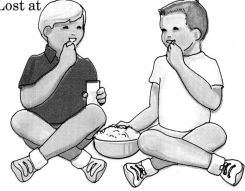

THE CACTUS LODE MINE

The old prospector's eyes sparkled and glistened
as around his campfire we sat and listened
to his story of lost gold
and how a mystery would unfold.

"Under the desert's sun one day
I almost became the buzzard's prey.
My burro Sam was by my side
while thirst for water parched my hide.

"Crawling through the scorching sand
I stumbled on, then tried to stand.
I knelt, then rose on wobbly knees
when on bright gold, my eyes did seize.

"I looked again, through blurry eyes
and saw five miners, half my size.
They gave me water and showed their treasure,
soon their story gave me pleasure.

"With nuggets golden, they loaded Sam,
filled my canteens and the packs did cram."
"Bring more burros to help us carry
our gold away, and please don't tarry!

"You'll come straight back to here,
if you take this cup, don't you fear.
Float cactus needles in the glass
this desert compass will find the pass."

"For nine years, all my time's been spent
following that needle where I am sent.
But just when I think I see the pass,
my thirst takes over, and I drink that glass.

"Day and night I sit and ponder
about that golden mine out yonder.
That treasure's there, if you care to follow
a cactus needle, but just don't swallow!"

FIND THE MINE GAME

Needs: Small stones, glue, gold glitter.

Rules

Make gold nugget place markers by painting one side of each stone with glue, dipping it in glitter and letting it dry. Then turn the stones over, paint the other side with glue and glitter, and let dry.

Put your marker on one of the start squares of the maze. Have a friend play too, by putting his or her marker on the other start square. Now, each of you close your eyes and bring your fist down on the palm of your hand twice, counting "One, Two." Then, bring your fist down again, saying "Three," and at the last minute straighten one, two or three fingers. The one with the least number of fingers showing gets to move that number of squares—or, if you both show the same number of fingers, you both get to move that number of squares.

Try to be the first one to get to the gold mine!

GOLD MINE GARDEN

Needs: Stones, sand, potting soil, miniature cactus plants, pretty flat dish, glue, gold glitter, plant food, water.

Instructions

Make gold nuggets in the same way as you did for the game, using some stones, glue and glitter. Then fill the bottom of the dish with potting soil, about 1–2 in. deep. Cover the soil with a layer of sand until all the potting soil is covered.

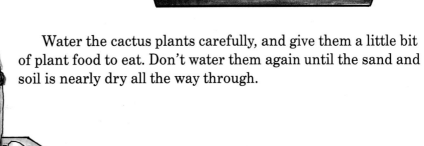

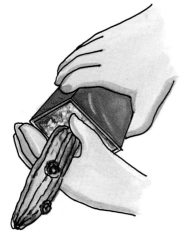

Next, carefully turn a cactus plant upside-down and tap the bottom of its pot. Be careful of sharp spines! If it doesn't come right out, have an adult help you take it out. Then dig a hole in the sand and soil, and plant the cactus. Use a little sand to cover any potting soil that shows.

Do the same for all the cactus plants. Next, pour sand between the cactus plants to make tiny sand dunes. Put in some bigger rocks, along with your gold nuggets to make the gold mine.

Water the cactus plants carefully, and give them a little bit of plant food to eat. Don't water them again until the sand and soil is nearly dry all the way through.

THE LANTERN
AND THE PRINCESS

Mai Lee was very pretty to see,
an oriental princess was she.
(Although she didn't want to be.)

Her servants took her everywhere,
never left her—they didn't dare!
She was always in their care.

How she longed to have her own place,
just a quiet, lovely, little space,
where she could paint and trace.

One special night, the moon shone bright,
and on the wall it made a sight,
a secret passage did it light.

She carefully peeked, so not to fall,
but couldn't see the way at all.
looking down that long, dark hall.

Taking her magic lantern flowers
she said the words that gave them powers:
and a glow arose that fell in showers.

She hurried down the secret way,
to a garden gate, "Oh I pray!"
Then opened it quickly, "Yes! Here I stay!"

The air was filled with heavenly scents
and moonlight gave a peaceful sense;
her heart's been quiet ever since.

Every evening to the garden she goes
but returns with morning, for she knows
to be a princess is the fate she chose.

ORIENT ISLAND PLANTER

Needs: Round or oval flat ceramic dish, potting soil, pebbles, bonsai juniper tree, scotch moss, water, stiff wire, plastic grafting tape, pliers.

Instructions

With your parent or an adult helper, visit a local nursery that has young juniper trees 4–8 in. high, suitable for training as a bonsai tree. Pick a tree that has an unusual shape.

At home, fill an oriental dish with potting soil so it is 2–3 in. deep. Plant the Juniper tree in the center of the dish and arrange the pebbles around it so they look like boulders around a real, full-sized tree.

Plant the moss so that it covers the potting soil like a green lawn, and water it gently so it starts to grow. Water again whenever the soil begins to dry out. Don't water too much or too often!

Train your Bonsai tree to be even more pretty by carefully bending its branches or trunk to follow a piece of twisted stiff wire, then taping it to the wire with grafting tape. After growing with the wire for a few months, it will keep its shape even when the wire is removed.

CHINESE LANTERN GARDEN

Needs: 2 ft. x 8 ft. flower bed, Chinese Lantern plant seeds, water hose.

Instructions

Chinese Lanterns are plants that have seed husks of bright orange. They make pretty winter dried flower decorations.

When spring weather warms, have an adult help you prepare the soil in the flower bed. Make a number of holes in the soil with 2 ft. between them. Then, plant 2 seeds in each hole. Push the seeds 1/4 in. into the ground and cover them with soil. Firm the soil with your hands.

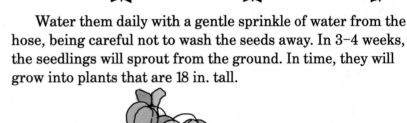

Water them daily with a gentle sprinkle of water from the hose, being careful not to wash the seeds away. In 3-4 weeks, the seedlings will sprout from the ground. In time, they will grow into plants that are 18 in. tall.

After the brightly colored husks turn orange, pick the stems and strip off the leaves. Hang them in a warm, dark place to dry. When they are completely dry, use them to make a table decoration for your house.

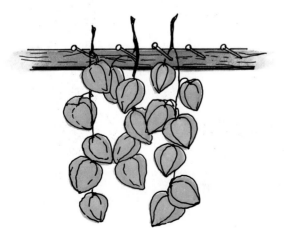

Snowflakes drifting from the skies
delighted Kim's excited eyes.
In early morning, she did rise
to build a snowman, just her size.

She made a friend, her very own,
colder than an ice cream cone.
She packed a snowball, rolled it round
Then another, on the ground.

She stacked them up, atop each other,
with a third ball, like a brother.
And, now that they were just as tall
she put a hat on top that ball.

She found a scarf, and twigs for arms,
and gray-blue rocks, his eyes did charm.
Corn husks were twisted for a smile,
while popcorn teeth took quite a while.

But from his face, still was missing,
the perfect nose, right for kissing!
To the snowy garden, then Kim went
to find a carrot, oh so bent.

Once her grandfather, now so old
explained the magic carrots hold.
So, digging in the frozen ground,
a perfect carrot soon was found.

Back to her snowman, Kim did run
with her carrot nose so fun.
And taking care to choose the place
she put that carrot on his face.

Imagine Kim's great surprise
when that snowman opened his eyes!
All that winter, they played around
until spring winds thawed out the ground.

CARROT BARNYARD

Needs: Pipe cleaners, toothpicks, colored markers, construction paper, scissors, glue, carrots with tops.

Instructions

Make a whole barnyard of colorful carrot characters.

Start by making a carrot horse: Wrap one pipe-cleaner around the carrot to make the front legs and another for the back legs—the carrot top makes the horse's tail. Draw and color your carrot horse's head with the colored markers, then cut it out and glue it onto the carrot. Draw, color, cut and glue a saddle, too!

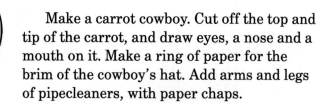

Make a carrot cowboy. Cut off the top and tip of the carrot, and draw eyes, a nose and a mouth on it. Make a ring of paper for the brim of the cowboy's hat. Add arms and legs of pipecleaners, with paper chaps.

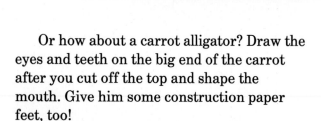

Or how about a carrot alligator? Draw the eyes and teeth on the big end of the carrot after you cut off the top and shape the mouth. Give him some construction paper feet, too!

Now that you've got the idea, use your imagination to make up lots of other animals and people!

CARROT PATCH

Needs: 3 ft. x 6 ft. garden plot, carrot seeds, watering can or hose.

Instructions

With a parent or adult helper, prepare the soil for your carrots (see pgs. 74–79 for help). Carrots come in lots of sizes and shapes, but they all like nice, loose soil to grow best. It's fun to grow several kinds.

Make a line in the soil by putting your rake upside down and pressing it into the soil, leaving a line about 1/4–1/2 in. deep. Then sprinkle your carrot seeds into the line, with the seeds about 1 1/2 in. apart. If you get a few seeds closer than that, don't worry—just pull out the extras when the seedlings have sprouted and have 3 leaves.

Carefully rake a little soil over the seeds and water them gently. Keep them damp until they sprout, usually in 2–3 weeks. In 2–3 months, you can start looking for your snowman's nose!

53

THE DRY DAY
RAINBOW

"My, oh my," Randy Rainbow said with a sigh.
"I cannot lie, but I wish I could cry!

"Look at Mr. Sun, out again today.
Mr. Cloud, please get big and gray
so you'll make him go away—
then I'll be able to go out and play!

"Children love me so, when all my colors glow.
After the rain away does go, I put on quite a show!"

But Mr. Cloud said, "I cannot come,
please try not to be so glum.
Instead look there, it'll cheer you some,
to see rosy red and a purple plum."

Yes indeed, it was true. Randy was no longer blue.
He saw colors there of every hue.

Children gardeners were having fun,
picking strawflowers one by one.
In the garden, with their bright flowers,
they looked like rainbows, without the showers.

"See Randy, they haven't forgotten you.
They have your colors on dry days, too!"

Now Randy is the happiest rainbow,
for he knows that our gardens glow
with all the colors that make us sigh
when he brightens up our sky.

DRYING AND PRESSING FLOWERS

Needs: Fresh garden flowers, silica gel, coffee can with lid, artifical stems, waxed paper, old magazines, books or bricks.

Instructions

You can keep your garden flowers forever by drying or pressing them. Let's try drying them first. Some flowers are easy. These are flowers that dry themselves—Strawflowers, Amaranth and Celosia are just a few. Cut their stalks, strip the leaves, and hang them upside down in a dark, dry place for 3-4 weeks.

Other flowers have too much moisture to dry that way. Pour some fresh silica gel (available at hobby stores) into a coffee can. Cut off your flower heads when they are nearly open and put them into the can with the gel. Then pour some more gel over them.

Cover the can with a tight lid and put it aside for a week or so. The gel will take all the moisture away from the flowers, leaving them dried out and pretty. Put each flower onto an artificial stem (also from the hobby store).

Press flowers, too! Pick them, being sure to cut below the first leaf. Put them on a sheet of waxed paper, then fold the paper over them like a sandwich. Carefully put them into a magazine, between the pages. Put some bricks or heavy books on top of them for 6-8 weeks. The flowers will flatten and dry out.

STRAWFLOWERS

Needs: 4 ft. x 6 ft. flower bed, Strawflower seeds, watering can or hose, florist's wire.

Instructions

Plant flowers that have crisp, straw-like petals even before they are dried! With an adult helper, prepare the soil (see pgs. 74–79 for help).

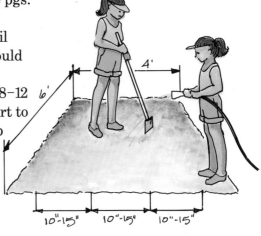

Strawflower seeds need light to sprout, so rake the soil smooth and scatter their seeds on top of it. Each seed should be about 10–15 in. from its neighbors.

Gently mist water onto the seeds. They will sprout in 8–12 days, then grow into tall plants 24–30 in. high. If they start to fall over, make a border fence of stakes and string to keep them in the bed.

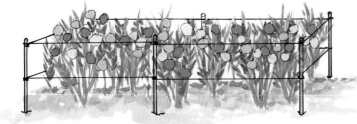

To keep your strawflowers, pick blooms that are just opening and stick a piece of florist's wire up through the stalk. Then hang them upside-down in a dark, dry place.

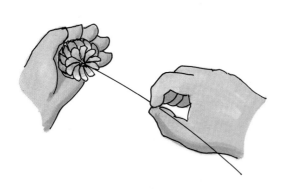

Who's hiding there, among that corn
behind green stalks, all forlorn?
Even though you're never seen,
we know you're hiding and where you've been!

You hide in there all through the night,
while we're safe, until first light,
but when we peek, we never see who —
we'd call your name, but we don't know you!

Some say you're a hobo, others a tramp
for all we know, it could be Gramps!
Why don't you come out here and play?
We're having fun sliding down our hay!

To tell the truth, we're a little scared.
Big kids tell stories about how they fared.
When they hunted for you down those rows,
about waving arms and torn clothes!

We may be brave, but we're not so bold
to push through corn, to take a hold
of tasseled stalks to hunt you down,
to run through rows and chase you round.

Oh, my goodness, don't we feel silly!
When we drew straws and sent in Billy,
and he bumped into your toe,
all he found was a silly scarecrow!

Our laughs and giggles we try to hide,
when younger kids are by our side
to ask who's in those tall corn rows,
but we don't tell them, no one knows!

HUNT FOR THE SCARECROW

Needs: 1 x 2 wood sticks, hammer, 1 1/2 in. finishing nails, rope, tin pie plates, string or twine, plastic or paper bag, colored markers.

Instructions

Here's fun for the whole neighborhood. Everybody looks around their houses for old clothes, caps, gloves, rags, sacks, shoes and nylon stockings or pantyhose for a scarecrow. Have your parents or an adult helper build a wooden frame with shoulders and legs that will go inside the clothes to hold them up.

Dress your scarecrow with pants, shoes, shirt and gloves for hands. Stuff it full of rags, newspaper, pantyhose or straw, until it's nice and plump. Make a belt out of the rope. Tie a pie plate to each hand.

For the head, stuff the bag or pantyhose until it is round and the right size, then put it on the wooden frame and tie it in place. Use the color markers to make eyes, nose and a funny mouth. Put its hat on, and your scarecrow is ready for the garden. The loose clothes and shiny pie plates will wave in the wind and keep the birds away from your corn!

CORNFIELD

Needs: 10 ft. x 10 ft. garden plot, corn seed, water hose.

Instructions

Corn grows tall and needs full sun all day long. Choose a good site and, with an adult helper, prepare the corn patch for planting (see pgs 74–79 for help).

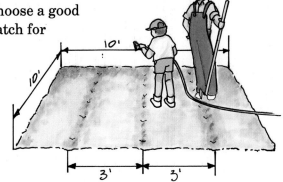

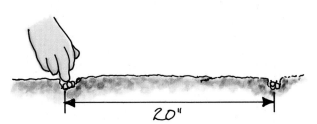

Plant your corn in short rows, side-by-side, making a square or block. Sow 3 seeds together in holes that are 20 in. apart, poking them into the soil with your finger about 1 1/2 in. deep. Each row should be 3 ft. from the next row. Water the corn each day until it sprouts, usually 7–10 days.

When the seedlings are 3 in. tall, pick the weakest seedling of each three, leaving 2 plants every 20 in. In about 3 months, your corn will be tall, with brown tassels and lots of yummy ears to eat!

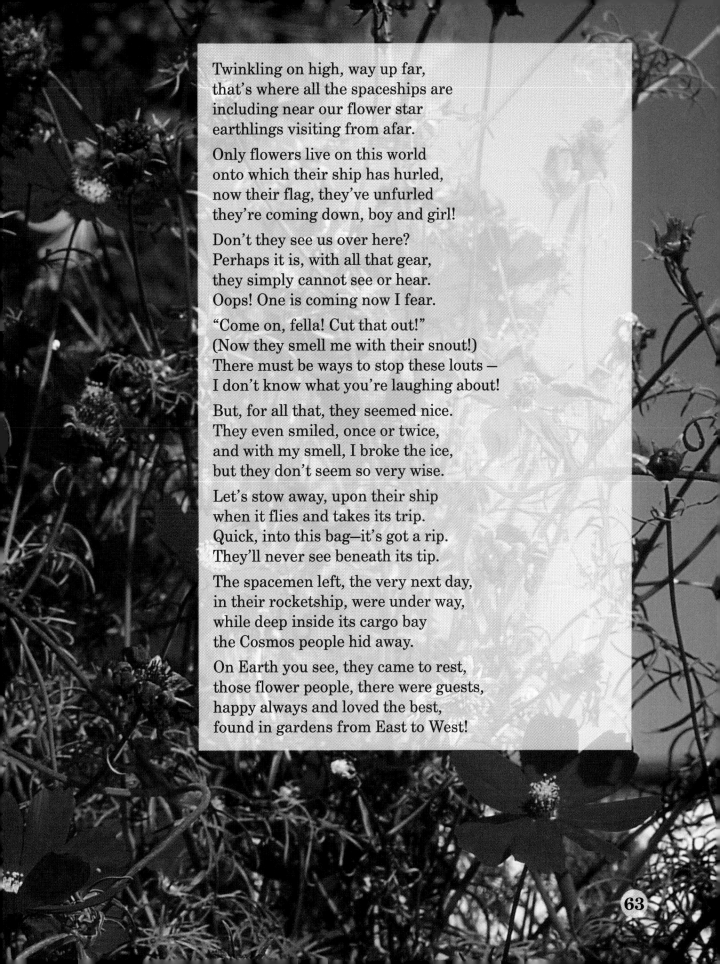

Twinkling on high, way up far,
that's where all the spaceships are
including near our flower star
earthlings visiting from afar.

Only flowers live on this world
onto which their ship has hurled,
now their flag, they've unfurled
they're coming down, boy and girl!

Don't they see us over here?
Perhaps it is, with all that gear,
they simply cannot see or hear.
Oops! One is coming now I fear.

"Come on, fella! Cut that out!"
(Now they smell me with their snout!)
There must be ways to stop these louts —
I don't know what you're laughing about!

But, for all that, they seemed nice.
They even smiled, once or twice,
and with my smell, I broke the ice,
but they don't seem so very wise.

Let's stow away, upon their ship
when it flies and takes its trip.
Quick, into this bag—it's got a rip.
They'll never see beneath its tip.

The spacemen left, the very next day,
in their rocketship, were under way,
while deep inside its cargo bay
the Cosmos people hid away.

On Earth you see, they came to rest,
those flower people, there were guests,
happy always and loved the best,
found in gardens from East to West!

COSMOS FLOWER PEOPLE

Needs: Tracing paper, pencil, crayons or colored markers, colored tissue paper, gummed paper stars, silver glitter, glue, pipe cleaners, scissors.

Instructions

Trace the flower people from the page onto your paper. Draw in the flower faces. Color them and give them names.

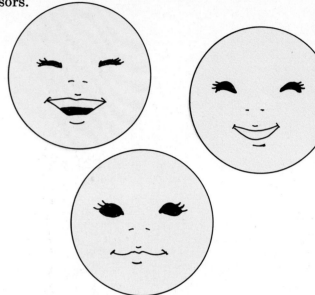

Using this circle as a guide, cut out colored tissue paper and crumple the pieces of tissue paper up into a ball, then smooth them out again. Then, carefully form them around your flower faces so that your flower people look out at you from within their paper "petals."

Glue stars and glitter on the tissue paper. Put each space flower on a pipe cleaner stem, so that you can make a space bouquet.

PLANTING COSMOS FLOWERS

Needs: 3 ft. x 8 ft. flower bed, Cosmos seeds, watering can or hose.

Instructions

Cosmos flowers like lots of sun, and they are as tall as most children! With your parent or an adult helper, prepare the ground for planting (see pgs. 74–79 for help).

Plant 2–3 seeds in each spot, about 12–15 in. apart. The seeds should be dropped onto the ground, then covered with 1/4 in. of soil. Sprinkle the dirt, then press it firmly down with your hands.

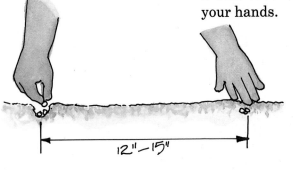

Water gently after planting, then every day until the seeds sprout (in 5–10 days). From then on, water whenever the soil dries.

Your flowers will bloom all season long. They also make nice decorations for your house.

Out in shade of the old apple tree
sat two dear friends, Mark and Laurie.
Above, in the branches, over their heads
were ripe red apples, and an owl that said,
WHO?

Goodness, they wondered, from where had it come,
they looked all around, then back to their chum.
They had just settled back, and returned to their talk
when the owl spoke again, with a loud, piercing squawk,
WHO?

This time they spoke, and called out their names,
"It wasn't us speaking, who's playing this game?
Is it you, Mr. Tree, who's teasing us so?"
Then the owl answered softly, so all would know,
WHO!

"A long time ago, there lived in this glen
a young boy named Johnny, who had a strong yen,
to travel the world, with a purpose in mind
to plant apple trees, for others to find."
WHY?

They asked owl, who looked down from above,
was it trees like this, that Johnny did love?
"No," said the owl, shifting his feet,
"It was children like you, that he'd never meet!"
WHY?

"Johnny loved apples, that's certain and true,
but the trees that he planted, he planted for you.
For the apples he loved, grew on a tree
that his father once planted, for him, you see!"
OH!

"Now this tree's grown old and is reaching its end
and the time's come to plant, all over again.
Go get your sapling, your spade and your cart,
You'll plant for YOUR children, and open your heart."
THAT'S WHO!

APPLE FACES

Needs: Apples, bleach soap, pencils.

Instructions

Old mountain people used to make apple head dolls for their children. These modern apple faces take some time and patience, but are fun and last for years. Start by choosing medium or small apples, from your tree or the store. Be sure to have a parent or adult helper wash them in cool soapy water with just a touch of liquid bleach added to it.

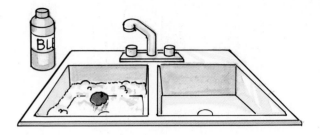

When you are done, put the apples into the warmest part of a frost-free refrigerator. In a few days, they will start to wrinkle just a little bit, as their moisture goes away. Take them out and start to work.

Press lightly with the pencil's eraser, pushing the apple's flesh in just a bit. Make an outline for the eye sockets, sides and bottom of the nose and along the underside of the mouth. Be sure not to break the apple's skin. Then put the apple back into the refrigerator for a few more days.

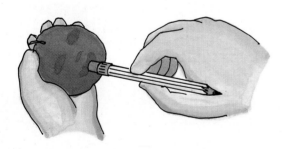

As the flesh of the apple shrinks, keep working it with the pencil eraser, making it into a wrinkled, old face. In about a month, you will have a real apple dollhead. If you want, you can even put it onto a doll's body and dress it like an old time man or woman.

PLANTING APPLE TREES

Needs: Planting site, shovel, bare-root apple tree, fertilizer, water hose, tree stake and tie.

Instructions

With a parent or adult helper, visit a nursery in the springtime. They have lots of different apple trees, ready to plant. Choose one that is good for your area and take it to the planting spot.

With the shovel, dig a hole twice as deep as the tree's roots and 1/2 again wider. Mix fertilizer with the soil from the hole, then build a cone out of soil in the bottom of the hole. This will support the tree's roots.

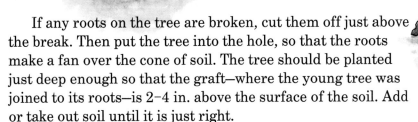

If any roots on the tree are broken, cut them off just above the break. Then put the tree into the hole, so that the roots make a fan over the cone of soil. The tree should be planted just deep enough so that the graft—where the young tree was joined to its roots—is 2–4 in. above the surface of the soil. Add or take out soil until it is just right.

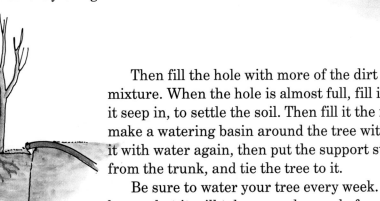

Then fill the hole with more of the dirt and fertilizer mixture. When the hole is almost full, fill it with water and let it seep in, to settle the soil. Then fill it the rest of the way, and make a watering basin around the tree with the extra dirt. Fill it with water again, then put the support stake in 6–10 in. from the trunk, and tie the tree to it.

Be sure to water your tree every week. It will soon sprout leaves, but it will take several years before it begins to produce apples.

OUTRIGGER ONA'A

70

On a sunny island, long ago,
by a deep, blue sea, in a valley low,
lived a boy named Ona'a, a brown-haired lad,
in a palm-frond hut, with his mom and dad.

While across the beach, in a calm lagoon,
gathered all his clan, where they soon
made their camp and began to fish,
for reef food was their favorite dish.

They launched canoes upon the waves,
carved from logs, they seemed so brave.
Ona'a dreamt of gliding, too,
when he saw their sleek canoes.

One day, along the ocean's beach
they sat and did young Ona'a teach.
They showed him how to carve tree wood
and paint it colors very good.

And when the boat was complete and done,
they let him paddle, just for fun.
For the first few minutes, in sun so bright
that canoe, for Ona'a, seemed right.

But Ona'a found that when he tipped
the canoe rolled sideways, and he slipped
into the water, with a splash,
his spirits daunted, but not his dash.

Then to his clan, he gave surprise
copying their ideas, oh so wise.
For on his canoe, two poles he lashed
with a log, to stop that splash.

Then he paddled everywhere
and fish he caught, with all he'd share.
On that beach, now called Kona,
his name became young Outrigger Ona'a.

POLYNESIAN TIKI MASK

Needs: Tracing paper, crayons or colored markers, scissors, glue and tape, feathers and shells.

Instructions

Become a Polynesian tiki! Trace the tiki's eyes, ears and mouth and color them with bright colors. Then cut them out, and glue the ears to a band of construction paper just big enough to fit around your forehead. Fold them up so that they stick out like real ears.

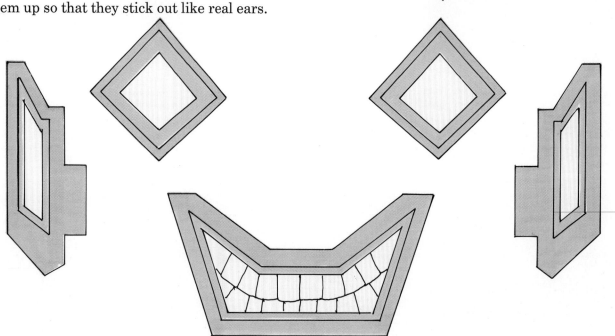

Then cut out and color a construction-paper circle the same size as your face with bright stripes where they will cover your cheeks. Carefully mark where your eyes will be on the mask and cut out holes so that you can see. Cut out the holes in the centers of the eyes that you colored, too. Glue the eyes and mouth onto the paper circle.

Next, tape the feathers onto the back of the oval so that they stick out above your hair. Glue a shell on for a nose. Then tape and glue the mask to your headband, and your mask will be ready to wear!

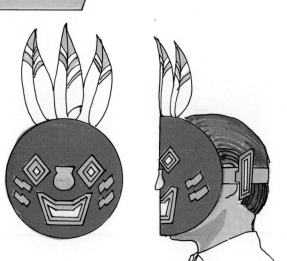

CUCUMBER OUTRIGGERS

Needs: Drinking straws, pencils, waterproof glue, cucumbers, knife, spoon, rubber bands.

Instructions

Make the outriggers by gluing 2 pencils to 2 straws, as shown. Set them aside to dry thoroughly.

With an adult helper, carefully slit the top off a big, straight cucumber. Then use a spoon to hollow the insides out of the cucumber—use it for your salads! This is the same way that some Polynesians used to create dugout canoes out of logs for fishing.

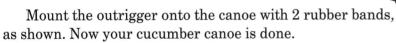

Mount the outrigger onto the canoe with 2 rubber bands, as shown. Now your cucumber canoe is done.

Race your canoe in a big pail of water, a shallow puddle or a wading pool. See who can blow their canoe across the pond first. If your canoe doesn't go straight, adjust the outriggers to help steer it.

GARDEN TIPS AND HINTS
GETTING READY TO PLANT

Before you can plant your seeds, the soil in your garden plot or flower bed must be just right.

With your parent, or an adult helper, and a shovel, you'll need to dig up and turn over all the soil in your plot. This gets rid of any weeds that have grown, and makes the soil loose and fluffy so that the roots of your plants can grow deep and strong.

Then sprinkle a layer of compost or fertilizer on the surface, and dig it in with the shovel and a rake.

Finally, to get the soil ready to plant, make the surface smooth by raking it with your rake. If there are still clods and clumps, hit them with the back of your shovel to smash them flat! Then rake some more, until the soil is flat and smooth.

Now, some plants need to grow in hills or mounds, while others like rows. A few just like to be sprinkled over a whole area. If you are going to plant your seeds by sprinkling them, you don't have to do anything else to the soil—just go right on to the next page and it will tell you how to plant!

But if you need to make a hill or row for your seeds, you'll need a hoe. Hills are easy. Just pull the dirt with the hoe all into one spot, about 12 in. around and 6-10 in. high. It's OK if you make a hollow around the hill—that's where the water will go when you water your plants!

For rows, work sideways with the hoe. Pull the soil up, making a furrow that is high in the middle and low on each side. To keep it straight, put a string between two stakes to follow as a guide.

Now that your soil is all ready for your seeds, go on to the next page, and we'll see how different seeds are planted!

When you finish digging and smoothing your plot, or making hills or rows, the soil should be damp, not dry or sticky.

Make a hill by hoeing soil into a mound 6–10 in. high and 12 in. around. Leave a basin around it for later watering.

Make a row by stretching string between 2 stakes. Use your hoe to move the soil from each side into the center under the string.

For seeds that you scatter on an area, rake it flat and smooth. Be sure to break up any clods of dirt that are left from digging!

GARDEN TIPS AND HINTS
PLANTING SEEDS

After the soil is all prepared for planting (see pgs. 74–75), you are ready to plant your seeds. Be sure to read all the instructions in the project before you start to plant. Have your parent or an adult helper read the directions on the seed package, too!

Planting seeds by scattering them in an area is easiest. Just pour the seeds from the package into your hand, and drop a few at a time so that they fall evenly onto the soil. Then rake them into the soil until they are covered (except the Strawflowers in the Forever Flowers project on pgs. 56–57—they just stay on top of the soil).

For planting rows, use the handle of your rake or hoe to make a line in the top of your furrow. Press it just as deep as the seeds should be planted. Then tap the seeds from the package into the line, and pinch the row closed with your fingers.

For planting mounds, put the seeds in a circle around the edge of the hill, about 2–3 in. from the edge. Then poke them into the dirt with your finger to the right depth, and sprinkle soil over them to cover them up. Finally, use your hands to press down on the whole mound and make the soil firm.

Sometimes it's easier to just plant little plants that your nursery or garden store has already grown. You should prepare the soil the same way as for seeds, then remove the plants carefully from their pots and plant them into a hole as big as their rootball. Be sure that they are only planted as deep as they grew in the pot!

When you finish seeding and planting, carefully water your seeds. They have to stay damp until they sprout, so water them at least once a day. But don't wash them out, and don't make it too wet—they'll rot!

Planting Mounds

To seed a mound, space the seeds evenly around the edge of the mound, then poke them into the soil with your finger.

Then sprinkle dirt into the holes and press down on the whole hill with your hands to firm the soil around the seeds.

Transplanting

For transplants, tip the container upside down and tap the plant out. Never pull it out by its stem!

Then, plant it—roots, dirt and all—into a hole the same size as the rootball. The rootball should be just under the soil.

Planting Areas

To seed an area, pour the seeds into your hand and scatter them over the area. Try to make the seeds fall as evenly as you can.

Then rake the seeds gently to cover them. Sprinkle soil over any seeds that still show, so all are covered up.

Planting Rows

To seed rows, use your rake or hoe handle to make a line in the top of the furrow. Tap the seeds from the package into it.

Then pinch the soil closed with your fingers to cover the seeds. Firm the soil by pressing down on it with your hands.

When your seeds and transplants are planted, water them gently by misting with a hose or a watering can. Don't wash out your seeds!

GARDEN TIPS AND HINTS
CARING FOR YOUR GARDEN

After your seeds have sprouted, you help them grow big, strong and healthy.

The most important care your plants need is regular watering. Healthy plants usually need to be watered every 4–7 days. You can tell when they need water by poking a trowel into the soil away from their roots. If it has dried out more than 2–3 in. below the surface, it's time to water.

When you water, give them a big drink, all at once, and let it soak in. Just sprinkling the surface won't do. If your plants have a water ditch around or alongside them, fill it up and let it soak in, then do the same again. That way the water will soak in deeply, and your plants will grow deep roots.

Some plants like to have drops of water sprinkle down from above, like rain. Others need to be watered from underneath, so that they aren't spoiled or catch a plant disease, called fungus. Water all your vines—watermelons, pumpkins and cucumbers—from beneath. Do the same for corn and most low flowers. Water carrots, bulbs and tall flowers from above or below, early in the day so all the water will dry off them before evening.

Besides watering, give your plants a little fertilizer every 3–4 weeks—ask your parent or adult helper what kind and how much. They'll read the label on the package to tell you! Fertilizer helps your plants be healthy, grow strong roots, and be tall. It also makes better flowers and bigger vegetables.

Weeding is also necessary. Wait until your plants are big enough to tell them from the weeds. Then pull the weeds out, or carefully hoe between the rows and mounds to cut them off at the roots.

Water by sprinkling flowers and tall vegetables with an overhead spray. Water early each morning so plants quickly dry.

Fertilize your plants every 3–4 weeks, using just as much as the package recommends. A balanced fertilizer—like 7–7–7—is best.

Water low-growing plants at their roots, keeping water off the plants' leaves. Water, let it soak in, then water again.

Weeds steal food and water from your plants. Pull them out by hand, being sure to get all of their roots. Take them out of the garden.

For small areas, use a watering can. Pour gently so that the soil isn't washed away or seeds are uncovered.

Hoe little weeds away, cutting them off at the roots or uprooting them completely. Be careful not to damage your plants!

A Note From
NK Lawn and Garden Co.

For more than 100 years, since its founding in Minneapolis, Minnesota, NK Lawn & Garden has provided gardeners with the finest quality seed and other garden products.

We doubt that our leaders, Jesse E. Northrup and Preston King, would recognize their seed company today, but gardeners everywhere in the U.S. still rely on NK Lawn & Garden's knowledge and experience at planting time.

We are pleased to be able to share this practical experience with you through this ongoing series of easy-to-use gardening books.

Here you'll find hundreds of years of gardening experience distilled into easy-to-understand text and step-by-step pictures. Every popular gardening subject is included.

As you use the information in these books, we hope you'll also try our lawn and garden products. They're available at your local garden retailer.

There's nothing more satisfying than a successful, beautiful garden. There's something special about the color of blooming flowers and the flavor of home-grown garden vegetables.

We understand how special you feel about growing things—and NK Lawn & Garden feels the same way, too. After all, we've been a friend to gardeners everywhere since 1884.